Piano Exercises Made Easy

by Gail Smith

© 2018 by Mel Bay Publications, Inc. All Rights Reserved.

WWW.MELBAY.COM

Preface

Exercises are essential for any type of training whether you want to be on a basketball team or play the piano. Our fingers can be trained to do amazing skills when good habits and continual practice take place. Our hand has 27 bones in each one, together making up ¼ of the entire body's bones.

This book combines learning to play the notes on the piano as you play each exercise. You will develop good fingering habits as you learn to press different combinations of notes, intervals and chords using the correct marked fingerings.

Talent combined with training is essential for success. Practice each exercise slowly then increase the speed. Each exercise has something new for you to learn. There are a variety of special exercises for gaining skill in sight-reading. One exercise has all 24 ways to play four notes and another is a special palindrome exercise with 120 ways to play five notes. These unique exercises will strengthen your eyes as well and your hands

Remember, only those who have the patience to do the simple things perfectly ever acquire the skill to do the difficult things easily. Some succeed because they are destined to. Most succeed because they are determined to.

I hope these exercises will be helpful on your musical journey.

GAIL SMITH

Contents

Exercise 1 - Thumb's Up	3
Exercise 2 - Index Fingerprint	3
Exercise 3 - Three Finger Waltz	4
Exercise 4 - My Four Ducks in a Row	4
Exercise 5 - A Big Mix-Up	5
Exercise 6 - The Sea Is at Low Tide	6
Exercise 7 - Just Walking Around	7
Exercise 8.1 - Three Palindrome Exercises Set #1A	8
Exercise 8.1 - Three Palindrome Exercises Set #1B	9
Exercise 8.2 - Three Palindrome Exercises Set #2A	10
Exercise 8.2 - Three Palindrome Exercises Set #2B	11
Exercise 8.3 - Three Palindrome Exercises Set #3A	12
Exercise 8.3 - Three Palindrome Exercises Set #3B	13
Exercise 9 - Turn on the Wipers; It's Raining	14
Exercise 10 - Mini Etude	15
Exercise 11 - Assorted Intervals	16
Exercise 12 - Handy	17
Exercise 13 - Wrist Action	18
Exercise 14 - Triple Play	19
Exercise 15 - Hanon's Famous Exercise	20
Exercise 16 - Half Steps	21
Exercise 17 - So ... Sew	22
Exercise 18 - Arpeggio Acrobat	23
Exercise 19 - Crossing Over the Keys	24
Exersise 20 - Hand Push-Ups	25
Exercise 21 - Triplet Drill	26
Exercise 22 - Inversion Drill	26
Exercise 23 - Chord Control	27
Exercise 24 - Chords and Their Inversions	27
Exercise 25 - Melodic Etude	28
Exercise 26 - Harmonic Etude	28
Exercise 27 - 12 Bar Exercise	29
Exercise 28 - Scales Are a Must	30
Exercise 29 - The Keys to Twelve Major Cities	32
Exercise 30 - Major Chord Exercise	35

Thumbs Up

1.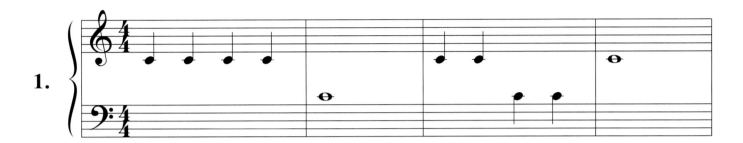

Index Fingerprint

2.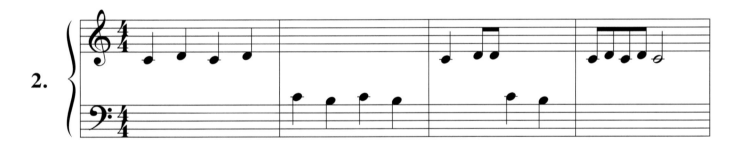

Three Finger Waltz

My Four Ducks in a Row

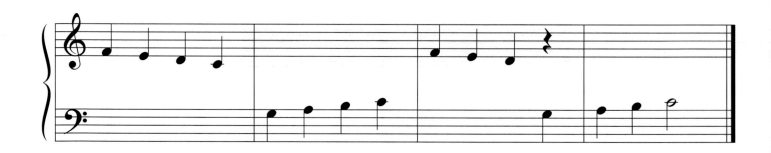

A Big Mix-Up

Sight-reading exercise for right hand only. When there are four notes, there are 24 different ways to play them. Here they are!

dedicated to Julian Mucci
The Sea Is at Low Tide
(The low C is tied)

Gail Smith

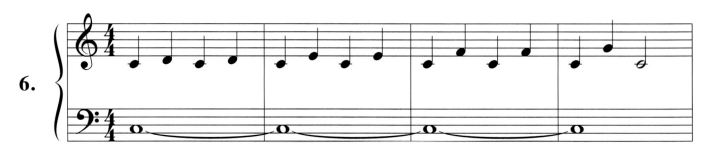

Just Walking Around

7.
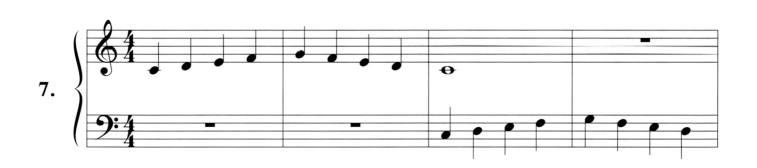

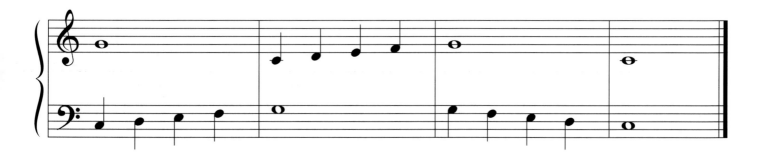

Three Palindrome Exercises
Set #1A

The 3 sets contain the 120 ways to play five notes. Each set is a complete palindrome. It is beneficial to exercise the eyes by playing the exercise backwards. It also improves sight-reading skills.

Gail Smith

Set #1B

Three Palindrome Exercises
Set #2A

The 3 sets contain the 120 ways to play five notes. Each set is a complete palindrome. It is beneficial to exercise the eyes by playing the exercise backwards. It also improves sight-reading skills.

Gail Smith

Set #2B

Three Palindrome Exercises
Set #3A

The 3 sets contain the 120 ways to play five notes. Each set is a complete palindrome. It is beneficial to exercise the eyes by playing the exercise backwards. It also improves sight-reading skills.

Gail Smith

Set #3B

Turn on the Wipers; It's Raining

Slow speed

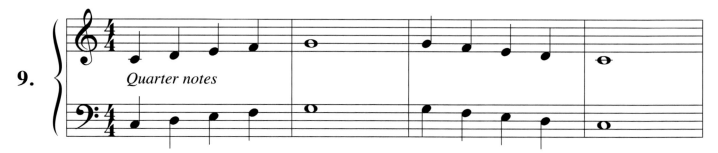

Fast speed

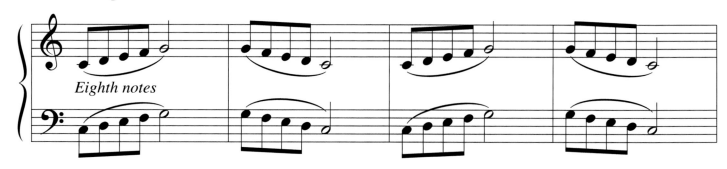

Faster speed

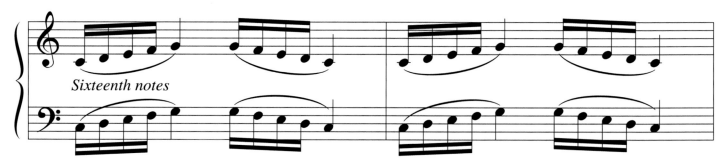

Fastest speed

Mini Etude

Gail Smith

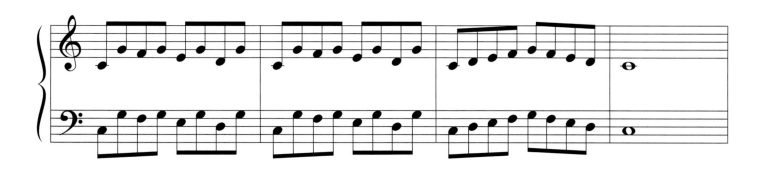
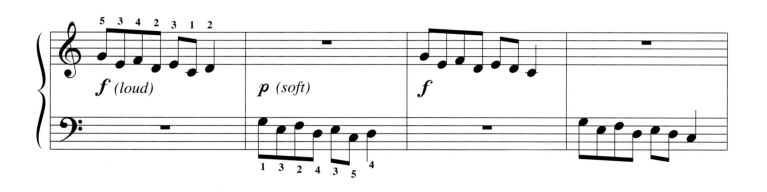

Assorted Intervals

Gail Smith

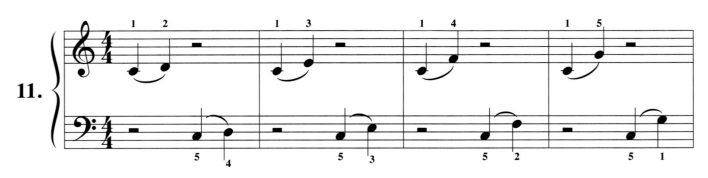
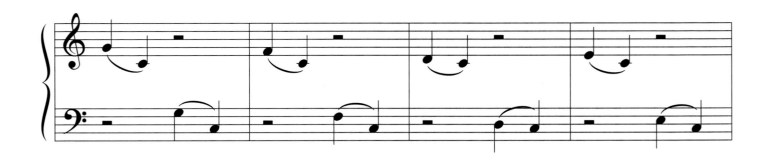
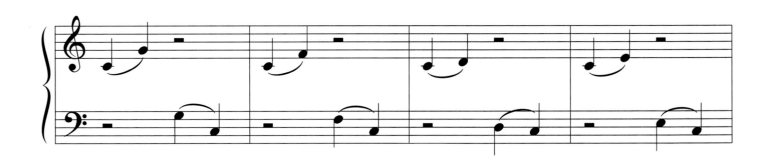

Handy
(Melodic Intervals, Harmonic Intervals)

Gail Smith

12.

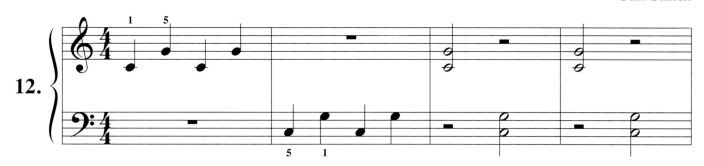

Wrist Action
(Down Up)

Gail Smith

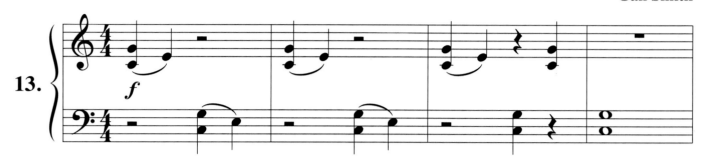
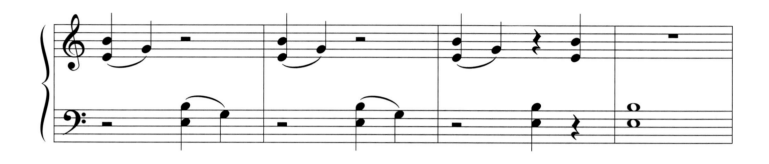
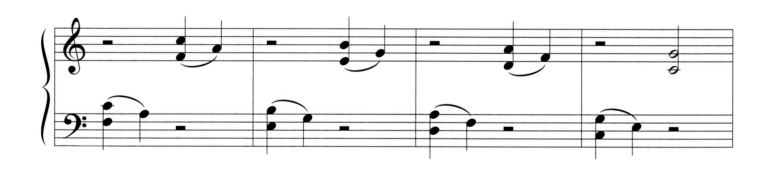

Triple Play
(Triplets and Triads)

Hanon's Famous Exercise

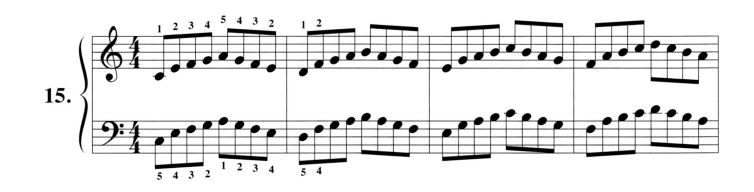

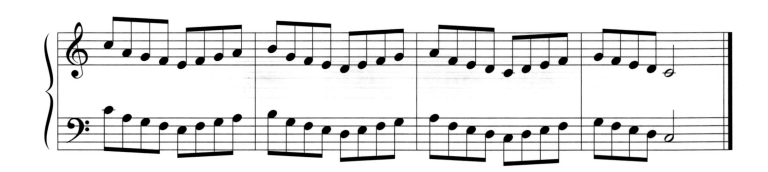

Half Steps
(The Chromatic Scale)

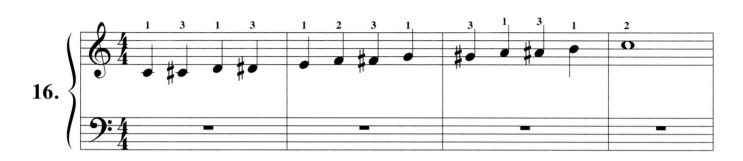

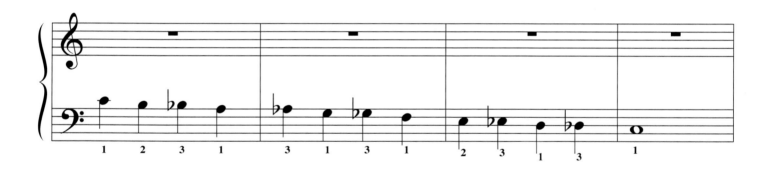

dedicated to Elise Case

SO ... SEW
Easy Enharmonic Etude
(Sounds the Same)

Gail Smith

Arpeggio Acrobat

Gail Smith

dedicated to James Case

Crossing Over the Keys

Gail Smith

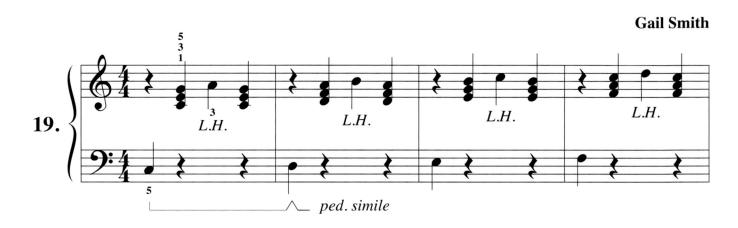
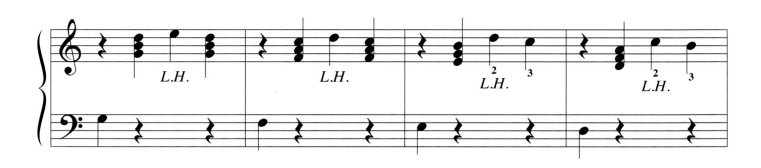

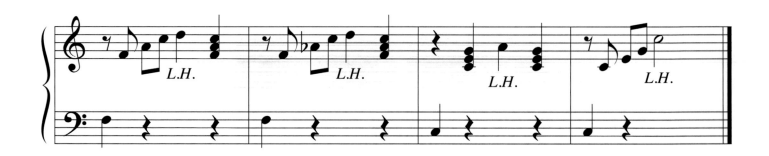

Hand Push-Ups

Gail Smith

Triplet Drill

Gail Smith

Inversion Drill

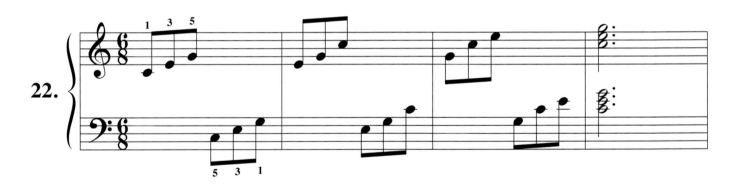
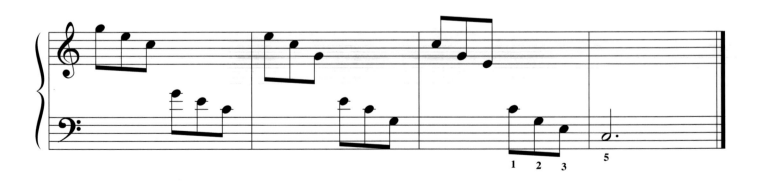

Chord Control
Jumping Chord Exercise

Chords and Their Inversions

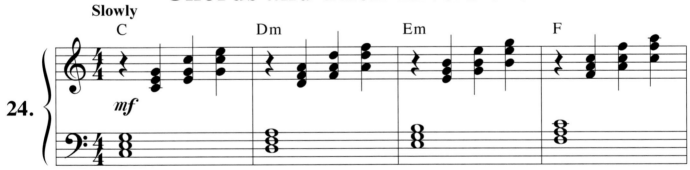

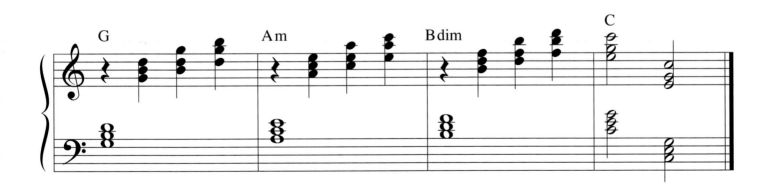

Melodic Etude

Gail Smith

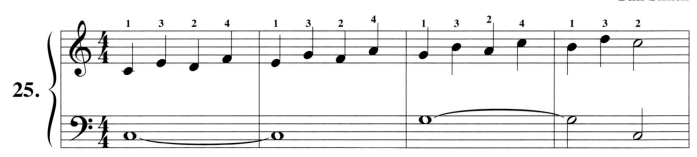
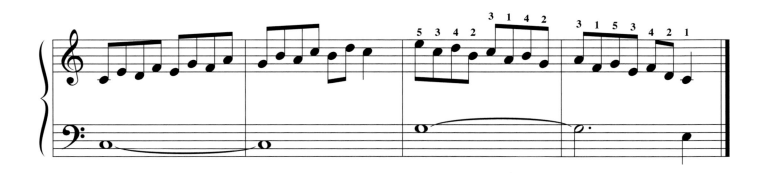

Harmonic Etude

Gail Smith

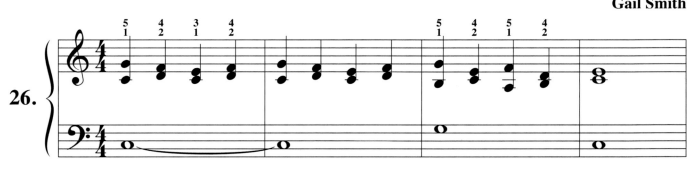

dedicated to Jasper Hooker
12 Bar Exercise

Gail Smith

Warm up

C Position

F Position

G Position

Scales Are a Must

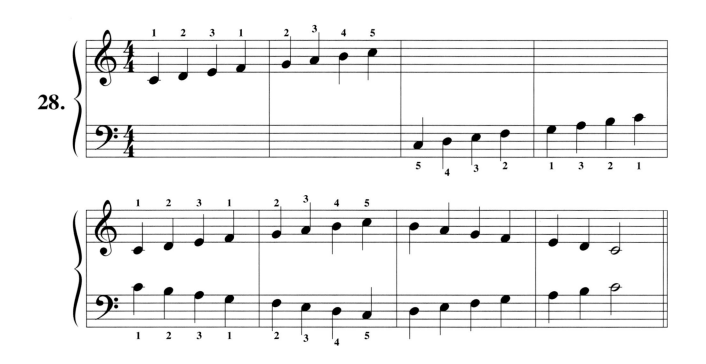

The following ten scales have the same fingering. It is easier to learn these ten scales first. Practice them hands-separately at first and then hands-together. Play them steady and smooth.

C Major **C Minor**

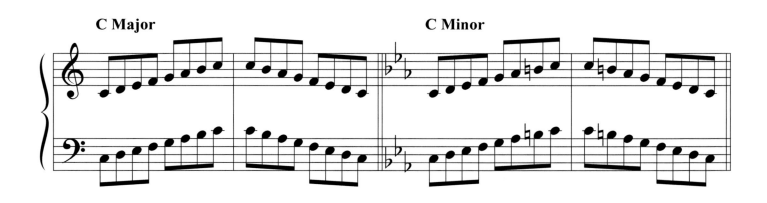

D Major **D Minor**

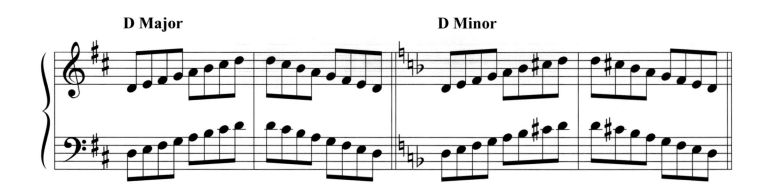

The Keys to Twelve Major Cities

This special exercise can be played without lifting your right hand from the piano keys. The order of the scales makes it possible for your fingers to go from one note to another, making it simple, smooth, and fun to run through all the scales.

Gail Smith

29.

C - Chicago

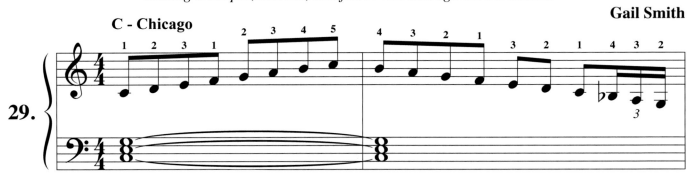

F - Fort Lauderdale

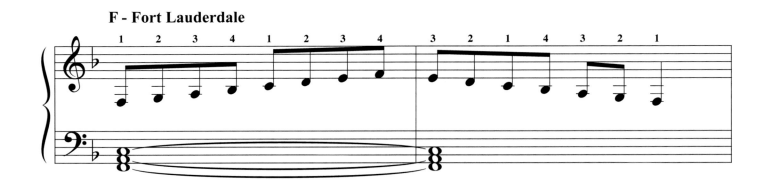

G♭ - Gainesville

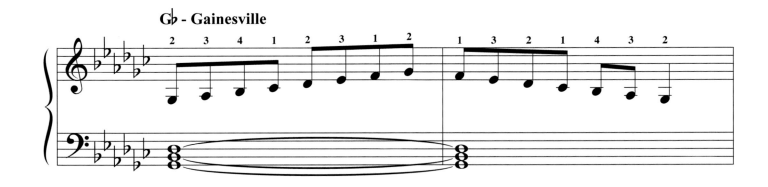

G - Grand Rapids

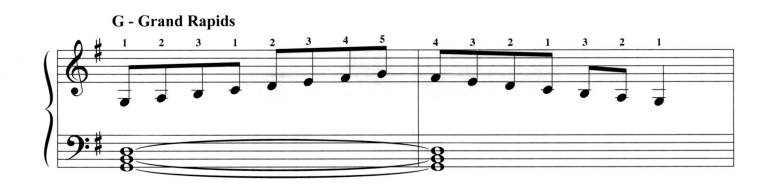

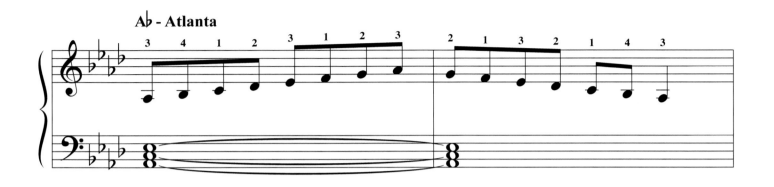
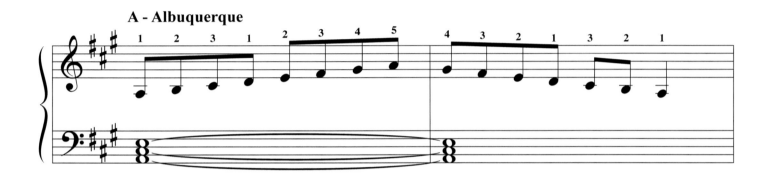
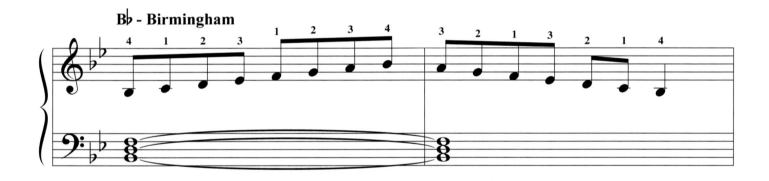
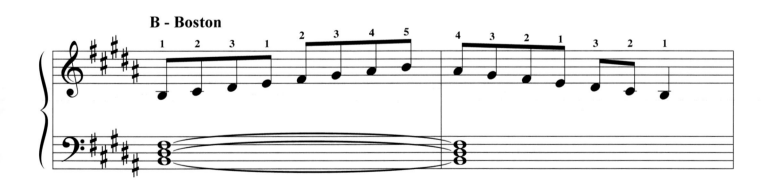

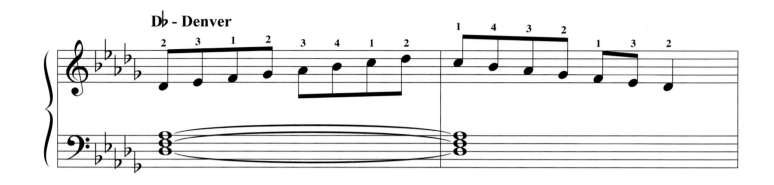

Db - Denver

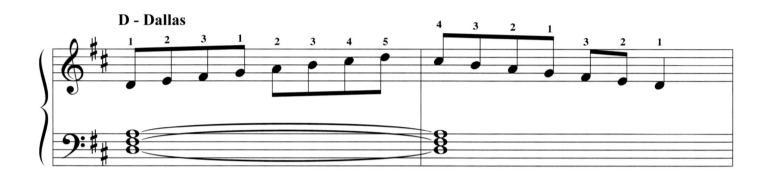

D - Dallas

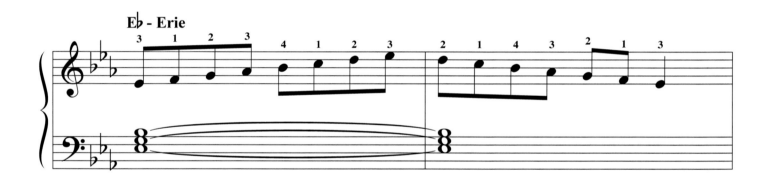

Eb - Erie

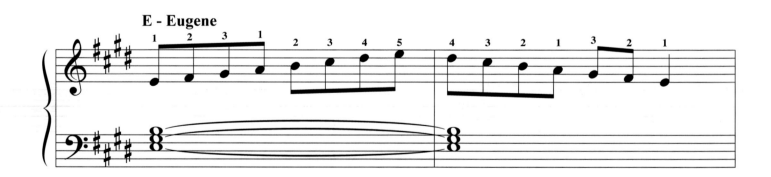

E - Eugene

Major Chord Exercise

Other Gail Smith Piano Books

Ten Waltzes by Johann Strauss, Jr. for Solo Piano
Canons and Rounds for Piano Solo
Country Gospel Piano Solos
Christian Classics for Piano Solo
Composing Made Easy
You Can Teach Yourself Gospel Piano
Great Literature for Piano Book 1 (Easy)
Great Literature for Piano Book 2 (Elementary)
Great Literature for Piano Book 3 (Intermediate)
Great Literature for Piano Book 4 (Difficult)
Piano Classics Made Easy
Beethoven Sonatas Book One
English Carols for Piano Solo
Native American Songs for Piano Solo
Complete Church Pianist
Complete Improvisation, Fills & Chord Progressions
Four Centuries of Women Composers
Hymns Made Easy for Piano Book 1
Hymns Made Easy for Piano Book 2
Hymns Made Easy for Piano Book 3
Palindromes for Piano
Patriotic Songs for Piano Made Easy
Complete Book of Exercises for the Pianist
12 Spirituals for Piano Solo
A Classic Christmas for Piano
Christmas Carols for Piano Made Easy
Classical Piano Solos for Worship Settings
Complete Book of Modulations for the Piano
Gospel Piano Made Easy
Patriotic Piano Solos
Piano Chords Made Easy
Piano Scales Made Easy
Piano for Seniors
Praise Piano Made Easy
Sunday Morning Pianist
Christmas Carols for Piano Made Easy
Celebrate the Piano Book 1 (Method)

WWW.MELBAY.COM